OCEAN MAMMALS

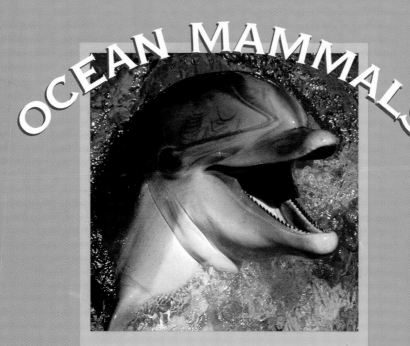

A TRUE BOOK

by

Elaine Landau

Children's Press®
A Division of Grolier Publishing
New York London Hong Kong Sydney
Danbury, Connecticut

For Michael, who loves the sea

Reading Consultant
Linda Cornwell
*Learning Resource Consultant
Indiana Department of
Education*

Subject Consultant
Kathy Carlstead, Ph.D.
*National Zoological Park
Smithsonian Institution*

The blue whale is the largest
animal on earth.

Library of Congress Cataloging-in-Publication Data

Landau, Elaine.
    Ocean mammals / by Elaine Landau.
        p. cm. — (A true book)
    Includes index.
    Summary: Discusses several different marine mammals including
dolphins, manatees, walruses, whales, and sea otters.
    ISBN 0-516-20041-0 (lib. bdg.)   ISBN 0-516-26110-X (pbk.)
    1. Marine mammals—Juvenile literature. [1. Marine mammals.
    2. Mammals.] I. Title. II. Series.
QL713.2.L36 1996
599.5—dc20   96-17885
                                          CIP
                                          AC

Contents

Fish are not the only creatures of the sea.

Ocean Mammals

Name an animal found in the sea. If you said a fish—of course, you are right. But other kinds of animals also live in these wet environments. Among them are ocean, or marine, mammals.

Some marine mammals may look like fish, but they are quite different. Marine mammals have larger and more well-developed brains than fish do. They also breathe differently. Fish use their gills to take oxygen from the water. Marine mammals, like humans, have

The fin whale breathes air at the water's surface.

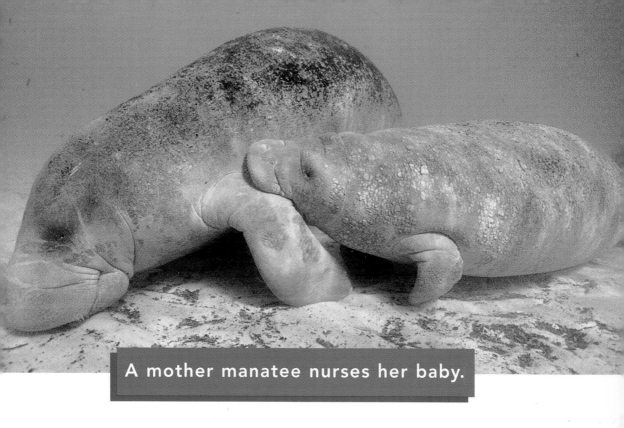

A mother manatee nurses her baby.

lungs. They must come to the surface of the water for air.

There are other differences, too. Marine mammals give birth to live young, and they nurse their newborns with mother's milk. Fish, on the other hand, reproduce by laying eggs.

The body temperatures of fish and mammals also differ. Most fish are cold-blooded— their body temperature changes according to how warm or cold their surroundings are. But marine mammals are warm-blooded—their body temperature stays about the same no matter what the temperature of their environment may be.

Humans must respect the many mammals living in the ocean.

This book looks at several fascinating marine mammals. There are many others like them in the sea. Many of these animals are in danger of dying out, however. Humans have proved to be their greatest enemy.

An

NORTH AMERICA

United States

Florida

Sea otters are presently found in the northern Pacific Ocean.

CENTRAL AMERICA

Walruses live in portions of the Arctic Ocean and the northern Atlantic and Pacific Oceans.

Atlantic Ocean

Caribbean Sea

A F

Pacific Ocean

SOUTH AMERICA

Manatees are found in the Caribbean Sea along the northeastern coast of South America and the coast of Western Africa, in Florida's bays and rivers, and in the coastal waters of the southeastern United States.

N
W · E
S

ANTA

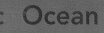

EUROPE

ASIA

AFRICA

Pacific
Ocean

Marine dolphins
are found in
nearly every ocean
of the world. River
dolphins are largely
found in Asia and
South America.

Indian Ocean

AUSTRALIA

Whales are
found in
every ocean
of the world.

ARCTICA

Bottlenose dolphins play in the water.

Dolphins

Nearly everyone has heard stories about dolphins and their special bond to people. They describe children riding on dolphins' backs or dolphins carrying swimmers safely to shore. More recently, ocean bathers have reported dolphins playfully nudging their legs.

There are many different kinds of dolphins. But all have torpedo-shaped bodies and long beaklike snouts. They breathe through a blowhole— a nostril on top of their heads. Dolphins have large brains and good vision. Their excellent hearing allows them to detect sounds that humans cannot hear.

The two main types of dolphins are marine dolphins and river dolphins. Marine

A dolphin breathes air through its blowhole.

dolphins are found in oceans or other bodies of salt water. River dolphins swim in either fresh or slightly salty water.

The best-known marine dolphins are the bottlenose dolphin and the common dolphin. Bottlenose dolphins are usually either black or slate-blue on top with a lighter underside. Their long snouts and curved mouths seem to form a smile. The bottlenose grows from 6 to 12 feet (1.8 to 3.7 meters) long and often stars in zoo and aquarium shows.

The common dolphin has a black back, white underside, and light stripes on its sides. Common dolphins frequently

follow ships at sea for miles—
leaping and somersaulting as
they swim along.

Common dolphins leap
together through the
vast ocean (above).
Bottlenose dolphins are
often used to entertain
in shows (right).

Although dolphins are admired by many people, their survival is still uncertain. In some parts of the world, dolphins are hunted for their meat. And many have died in

Beginning in the 1980s, fishing nets are designed to help save dolphins.

Scientists learn more about dolphins by studying how they communicate.

fishing nets that were meant to snare tuna and other fish. In 1990, major U.S. tuna-canning companies refused to buy tuna caught in nets that are harmful to dolphins. As a result, the number of dolphins drowned in fishing nets has decreased.

Manatees

The manatee is a slow-moving sea mammal. Depending on the species, manatees measure 8 to 12 feet (2.4 to 3.7 m) long and weigh 440 to 1,320 pounds (200 to 600 kilograms). While manatees may look a lot like whales, they are not closely related to them.

The manatee's paddle-shaped tail helps it swim (above). At times, manatees have been helpful to humans by eating excessive plants (right). They have kept canals open that might have become clogged.

A manatee's closest relative is the elephant!

Manatees live on various water plants, including sea-weed and grasses. Many of these plants contain tough needles that wear down their teeth. A manatee's teeth are continuously replaced, however. The animal's constant chewing causes its teeth to slowly move forward along its jaws. New teeth come from the back to replace its worn-out front teeth. Manatees need strong teeth because they spend from six to eight hours a day eating. The average manatee eats 55 to 95 pounds (25 to 43 kg) of food daily.

Young calves stay with their mothers.

Manatees usually live alone, though two or three of them sometimes remain together. The most lasting bond occurs between mother manatees and their newborn calves. The two stay close to each other for about two years.

The gentle manatee has no natural enemies, but humans have threatened its survival. Manatees have often been killed for their tasty meat, and their body oil is used for cooking. Even in areas where they are not hunted, manatees are in danger. They often get in the way of motorboat propellers, and they are sometimes injured by barges and canal locks. Today, there are only about 1,800 manatees left in the United States.

A boat's propellers scarred the back of this manatee (above). Signs help to warn boaters of manatees in the area (left).

CAUTION

MANATEE AREA

This young walrus has not yet grown its long tusks.

Walruses

The walrus, a massive reddish-brown sea mammal, is actually an oversized seal. Walruses grow up to 12 feet (3.7 m) long and weigh as much as 3,000 pounds (1,360 kg).

A walrus has tiny eyes, a head that looks too small for its body, and wrinkled skin. Its

Walruses crowd on top of a large rock (left). Walruses rest on an ice floe (right).

hands and feet are flippers, and two long ivory tusks add to its unusual appearance.

Walruses prefer the shallower waters near the coastline where there are clams, mussels, snails, and crabs to eat. These marine

mammals are usually found
in areas where ice floes are
common. They often climb
on these floating blocks of
ice to rest at a safe distance

A herd of walruses in Alaska

Walruses have long been hunted for their tusks. Eskimos are among the only people still allowed to hunt walruses.

from their predators, such as polar bears.

Walruses like company. They live in herds of up to

about one hundred animals. Even when there is enough room for them to stretch out by themselves, walruses lie touching or on top of each other.

Through the years, the number of these animals decreased as humans hunted walruses for their ivory tusks and the oil from their blubber. Russia, Norway, Canada, and the United States have now passed laws that ban walrus hunting.

Whales

Whales are large, intelligent marine mammals. There are many different kinds of whales. Some are huge. The blue whale, for example, at almost 100 feet (30 m) long, is the largest animal on earth. Some whales are small, like the beluga whale, which

The tail above belongs to a mighty blue whale. Compared to the blue whale, the beluga whale (right) is quite small.

measures only 10 to 15 feet (3 to 4.5 m).

Scientists divide the various types of whales into two main groups—baleen or toothless whales and toothed whales. All whales are alike in some ways,

A beluga mother and her young (above); people get a close up view of a toothless gray whale (left).

however. For example, they have no sense of smell. They rely on their hearing, which is superior to that of humans.

A whale usually gives birth to a single offspring at a time. Sometimes, other females assist the mother in giving birth. Even a newborn whale is a large animal. Despite its massive size, a young whale remains with its mother for about a year.

Many types of whales travel long distances together in herds. They communicate with each other by a variety of sounds. These noises may

A herd of humpback whales in Alaska (left) and a herd of beluga whales in Canada (right).

help them keep track of each other on their journeys.

Humans have long been the whale's greatest predator. Even though all nations banned commercial whaling by the late 1980s, these regulations were often ignored. By the early 1990s, some nations relaxed their rules and permitted some kinds of whales to be hunted. The United States, however, continues to ban commercial whaling and importing whale products.

Commercial whaling was banned so that whales, like this orca, can roam safely in their ocean habitat.

Sea otters float on the water.

Sea Otters

The sea otter is a furry, dark brown sea mammal. It measures 4 to 5 feet (1.2 to 1.5 m) long and weighs up to 85 pounds (39 kg). Sea otters have wide, flat heads and flipperlike hind feet.

These animals live in the water and feed on a variety of

Sea otters use rocks to crack open shellfish.

marine life, including crayfish, octopuses, crabs, squids, mussels, crabs, clams, and fish. They float on their backs while eating or even nursing their young. A sea otter sleeps in the water by wrapping seaweed around its body. This keeps the animal from drifting out to sea.

The family groups of these animals are made up of females and their young. Males usually live alone nearby. Sea

A sea otter wrapped in seaweed

otters spend a good deal of time playfully romping with one another in the water. In captivity, they adjust well to humans. They will even take food from a person's hand.

A mother sea otter and her baby

Sea otters live together in seaweed-filled coves.

At one time, sea otters were plentiful. But they were hunted to the point of near-extinction for their valuable fur. Today, sea otters are legally protected throughout the world.

To Find Out More

Here are more places to learn about ocean mammals:

 **Books**

Arnold, Caroline. **Sea Lion.** Morrow Junior Books, 1994.

Arnosky, Jim. **Otters Under Water.** G.P. Putnam, 1992.

Burnie, David. **Seashore.** Dorling Kindersley, 1994.

Carrick, Carol. **Whaling Days.** Clarion Books, 1993.

Cossi, Olga. **Harp Seals.** Carolrhoda Books, 1991.

Darling, Kathy. **Walrus: On Location.** Lothrop, Lee & Shepard Books, 1991.

Kraus, Scott, D. **The Search for the Right Whale.** Crown, 1993.

McMillan, Bruce. **Going on a Whale Hunt.** Scholastic, 1992.

Sobol, Richard. **Seal Journey.** Cobblehill Books, 1993.

 **Organizations**

American Zoo and Aquarium Association
7979-D Old Georgetown Rd.
Bethesda, MD 20814
(301) 907-7777
http://www.aza.org/

Sea World of California
Education Department
1720 South Shores Rd.
San Diego, CA 92109-7995
(619) 226-3834

Sea World of Florida
Education Department
7007 Sea World Drive
Orlando, FL 32821-8097
(407) 363-2380

**Zoological Society
of San Diego**
P.O. Box 271
San Diego, CA 92112-0271
http://www.sandiegozoo.org/

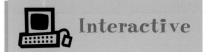

**Mammals: A Multimedia
Encyclopedia.** National
Geographic Society.
Discover photos, videos,
and sounds of hundreds of
mammals—from aardvarks
to zebras! Ages 7+

Animal Bytes: Walrus
http://www.bev.net/
education/SeaWorld/
animal_bytes/walrusab.html
Learn where walrus live, what
they eat, and a lot more.

Manatee Home Page
http://cns-web.bu.edu/
pub/soddo/manatee.html
Unearth great photos and
information on these
friendly marine mammals.

The Otter Page
http://mathssun5.lancs.ac.
uk.2080/~maa017/Otters/
otters.html
Otters are one of the
world's cutest and smartest
mammals. See for yourself!

**Whales: A Thematic
Web Unit**
http://curry.edschool.virginia.
edu/~kpj5e/Whales
Explore this wonderful
resource filled with
projects, lessons, whale
research, and more!

Important Words

blowhole opening in the heads of dolphins and whales that allows them to breathe

blubber the fat of large marine animals

calves newborn young

captivity having been captured and held

extinction no longer existing

flipper a sea animal's flattened limb, used for swimming

gills the organ of a fish that absorbs dissolved oxygen from the water

herd a group of animals

ice floe a large piece of floating ice

predator an animal that lives by hunting other animals

snare to trap or capture

species a particular type of animal

Index

Meet the Author

Elaine Landau worked as a newspaper reporter, children's book editor, and youth services librarian before becoming a full-time writer. She has written more than ninety books for young people.

Ms. Landau thinks that many ocean mammals are among the earth's most marvelous creatures. On a recent cruise to Alaska, she spent much of her time whale watching.